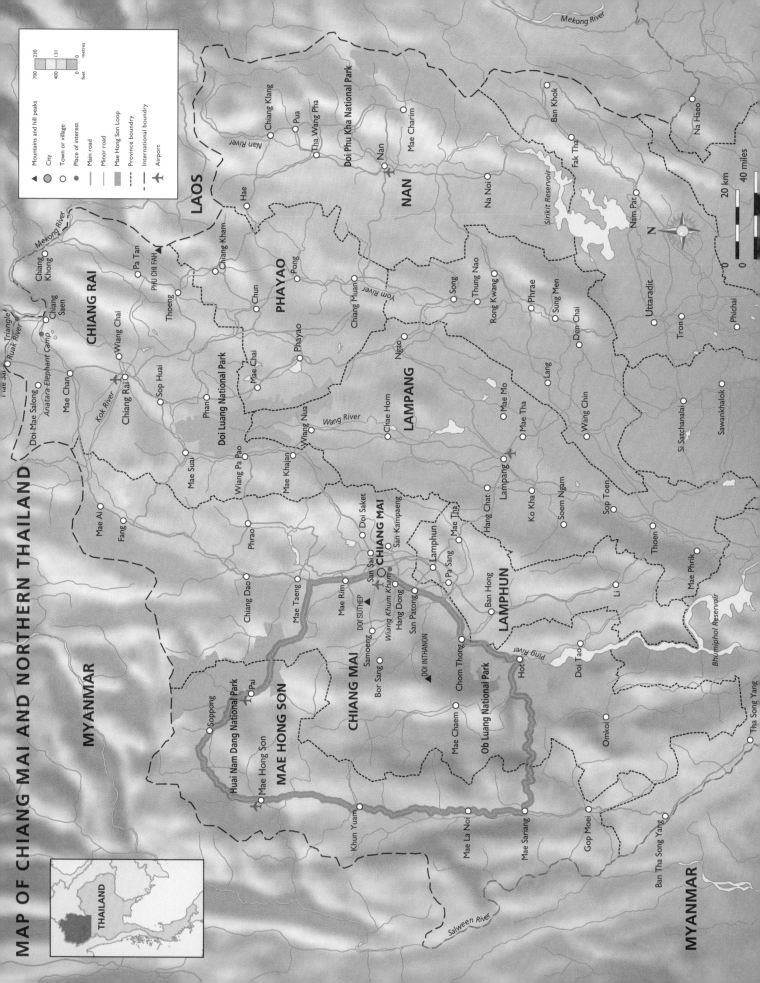

MAP OF CHIANG MAI AND NORTHERN THAILAND

Mountains and hill peaks
City
Town or village
Place of interest
Main road
Minor road
Mae Hong Son Loop
Province boundry
International boundry
Airport

metres
700   230
400   131
0   0
feet

THAILAND

20 km   40 miles
0   0

N

LAOS

MYANMAR

MYANMAR

CHIANG RAI

NAN

PHAYAO

LAMPANG

CHIANG MAI

MAE HONG SON

LAMPHUN

Mekong River

Mekong River

Ruak River

Golden Triangle

Chiang Khong

Chiang Saen

Doi Mae Salong

Anatara Elephant Camp

Mae Chan

Kok River

Chiang Rai

Wiang Chai

Sop Huai

Phan

Mae Suai

Wiang Pa Pao

Mae Khajan

Mae Ai

Fang

Phrao

Chiang Dao

Chiang Mai Phu Chi Fah National Park

PHU CHI FAH

Pa Tan

Thoeng

Chiang Kham

Hae

Chiang Klang

Pua

Tha Wang Pha

Doi Phu Kha National Park

Nan

Mae Charim

Na Noi

Sirikit Reservoir

Ban Khok

Fak Tha

Nam Pat

Na Haeo

Phichai

Tron

Uttaradit

Si Satchanalai

Sawankhalok

Phrae

Den Chai

Sung Men

Lang

Wang Chin

Thoen

Mae Phrik

Mae Prik

Thoen

Sop Toen

Soem Ngam

Ko Kha

Lampang

Hang Chat

Mae Tha

Mae Mo

Rong Kwang

Song

Thung Nao

Phong

Chun

Chiang Muan

Phayao

Yom River

Ngao

Chae Hom

Wang River

Wiang Nua

Doi Luang National Park

Mae Chai

Nan River

Nan River

Doi Saket

San Sai

San Kampaeng

Bor Sang

Samoeng

DOI SUTHEP

Wiang Khum Kham

Hang Dong

San Patong

DOI INTHANON

Chom Thong

Mae Chaem

Ob Luang National Park

Hot

Doi Tao

Omkoi

Ping River

Bhumiphol Reservoir

Tha Song Yang

Gop Moei

Mae Sariang

Mae La Noi

Khun Yuam

Mae Hong Son

Huai Nam Dang National Park

Soppong

Pai

Mae Taeng

Mae Rim

Lamphun

Pa Sang

Mae Tha

Ban Hong

Li

Ban Tha Song Yang

Salween River

Mae Chan

Mekong River

ENCHANTING

CHIANG MAI

& NORTHERN THAILAND

MICK SHIPPEN

Contents

Above: Lampang is renowned for its horse-and-cart taxis.

Above centre: Once a remote town, Mae Hong Son is now a popular base from which to go trekking in the surrounding mountains.

Above left: Craftsmen and women in Bor Sang make beautiful umbrellas and parasols from bamboo and handmade paper.

Opposite: Chiang Rai features an ornate clock tower and main streets lined with golden, Lanna-style lamp posts.

Title page: A detail of the silver temple, Wat Sri Suphan in Chiang Mai.

Chapter 1:
An Inspiring Destination

Chiang Mai, Thailand's second city and capital of the former Lanna kingdom, is the gateway to the mountainous north. For decades, the city has been the starting point for travellers in search of exotic hill tribes, the adventure of trekking, kayaking, cycling and rafting, and more restful pursuits, such as bird watching, meditation or learning Thai massage or Thai cooking.

Mention Chiang Mai and many travellers conjure up an image of a peaceful historic city encircled by mountains where life proceeds at a more sedate pace than elsewhere in Thailand, not least because for years it was known as the 'Rose of the North'. It is no wonder, then, that most first-time visitors are surprised when they arrive in a burgeoning city with a population that exceeds one million people in the metropolitan area.

Yes, Chiang Mai enjoys an impressive mountain backdrop, its streets and moats are tree-lined, it is home to numerous ancient temples and bustling fresh food markets, and there is a certain easygoing charm to northern Thai

Left: Northern Thai temples often feature exquisitely carved wooden doors painted red and gold.

Opposite top: Forest-covered northern Thailand attracts birdwatchers from around the world who come to see the migratory birds that arrive during the cool season. This male White-rumped Shama, is a resident species that inhabits forests up to 1500 m (5.000 ft).

Opposite below: Artisans in Chiang Mai produce a wide range of crafts and homeware and there are many colourful boutiques and galleries to explore especially in the Nimmanhaemin Road area.

Below: The Anantara Chiang Mai Resort, a chic, contemporary Lanna-style hotel in the heart of Chiang Mai.

people but in recent years the city has undergone rapid expansion and renovation, shaking off the last remnants of its backpacker image to re-emerge as the new capital of Lanna chic and a destination for sophisticated travellers.

Today's Chiang Mai is renowned for unique hotels, trendy boutiques full of high-quality products created by talented local artisans and riverside restaurants where diners can enjoy the distinctive northern cuisine under the stars.

Despite the welcome makeover, Chiang Mai's fascinating history is still a major attraction. Down the narrow winding lanes of the historic district within the boundaries of the old city wall there is great pleasure to be found uncovering gems, such as the city's oldest temple, Wat Chiang Man, riding in a pony and trap around the ruins of Wiang Khum Kham or making a pilgrimage to the most famous temple of all, Wat Phra That Doi Suthep, which crowns the 1,676-m (5,500-ft) Suthep mountain and offers panoramic views of the city below.

Beyond the city, adventure awaits. The surrounding provinces are undoubtedly some of Thailand's most picturesque and least visited. Chiang Mai Province itself is home to Doi Inthanon, the country's highest peak. Crowned by twin pagodas, it acts as a beacon to Bangkokians in the cooler months, drawing them up the mountain in droves to experience the brief but invigorating winter chill. Head north from the city and a road known to motorcyclists as the 'Mae Hong Son Loop' takes travellers on a 600-km (373-mile) rollercoaster ride through the town of Pai, on to the caving centre of Soppong and the loop's namesake, the lovely Tai Yai-influenced town of Mae Hong Son, before snaking south to Mae Sariang and back to Chiang Mai.

Chiang Rai and the infamous Golden Triangle still cast a spell on visitors. These days, however, the lure is not opium but tea plantations, inspirational royal projects, idyllic resorts and boat trips down the mighty Mekong River. For those prepared to go the extra mile, there are also charming northern towns, such as Nan which sits in the shadow of Doi Phu Kha National Park, and the picturesque lakeside town of Phayao.

Chiang Mai with the distinctive culture and lush landscape of the north is set apart from the rest of Thailand. Vibrant and confident, modern-day Chiang Mai is alive with creativity, making it an exciting destination for even the most fashionable of globetrotters. For lovers of culture and the great outdoors, the region offers beauty and insight for a rewarding travel experience.

Left: Ob Luang is a 300-m (1,000-ft) canyon on the edge of Ob Luang National Park and one of many natural attractions that draw visitors to the north. It is possible to camp at the water's edge and explore the park on a trek.

Geography and Climate

The north of Thailand is a mountainous, forest-covered region bordering Myanmar and Laos that encompasses 17 provinces including Chiang Mai, Chiang Rai, Nan, Mae Hong Son, Phayao, Lampang and Lamphun covered here.

The western frontier runs from Tak Province upward to Mae Hong Son and some districts of Chiang Mai and Chiang Rai while to the east the border with Laos is demarcated by mountain ranges from Phetchabun up through Uttaradit, Nan, Phayao and Chiang Rai. In Chiang Saen and Chiang Khong districts the border with Laos is formed by a 90-km (56-mile) stretch of the Mekong River.

Covering an area of 169,644 km^2 (65,500 sq miles), northern Thailand is 40 per cent forest, although much of this is secondary growth following years of logging. In areas such as Nan, deforestation has been particularly heavy, where trees have been replaced by cash crops such as sweetcorn. More than ten per cent of land is given over to agriculture and farming flourishes in the fertile valleys. The area produces much of Thailand's fruit and vegetables.

Right: Although Chiang Mai and Mae Hong Son are linked by air, the journey by road is worth taking as it passes through mile after mile of beautiful mountain scenery. There are also many interesting places to stop along the route.

The north's many hill tribes are also engaged in farming on mountain slopes. In the past they were slash-and-burn farmers who would move on once the land's nutrients had been exhausted but this practice was stopped by King Bhumibol who instigated several royal projects in the 1960s to encourage a more settled way of life and provide a real and sustainable alternative to the opium cultivation that blighted the area. However, the clearing of land with fire is still a major problem in the north and during the months of February and March the area is often blanketed in a choking smoky haze.

Twenty-three areas of outstanding beauty in the north are designated national parks. These include Doi Inthanon National Park, home to the country's highest and most visited mountain, and Ob Luang National Park, which features a 300-m (1000-ft) long canyon. Northern Thailand is the source of several important rivers including the Ping that flows through Chiang Mai, as well as the Wang, Yom and Nan that converge at Nakhon Sawan to form the Chao Phraya River.

In the hills and valleys of Mae Hong Son from early November until mid-December one of Thailand's most unspoiled scenic areas turns to gold as the wild Mexican sunflowers come into bloom. Doi Mae U-kor mountain peak in the Khun Yuam district of Mae Hong Son is considered to be the best location to enjoy the spectacle of the seasonal display known locally as *dok bua tong* or golden flowers.

The northern provincial capital of Chiang Mai lies 800 km (500 miles) north of Bangkok and just over an hour away by air. The fertile valley in which it lies is 310 m (1,017 ft) above sea level. Chiang Mai is the major transport, education and cultural centre for the region and the thriving city acts as a magnet for many northerners who come in search of work.

In keeping with the rest of the country, the north has three seasons but the cool season is more pronounced. During the hot season from March to May temperatures can reach 38°C (100°F) or higher. The rainy season begins in June, gradually building to a peak in September and October. The most pleasant months are from November to February when mornings and evenings can be very chilly but it is still hot in the afternoon. Chiang Mai and northern Thailand are year-round destinations but attract most visitors during the cool season and for major festivals scattered throughout the year (see pages 24 to 27).

This page: Rice is the staple grain of Thailand. In the northern province of Phayao, the valley floors are carpeted with rice 'padis'. Seedlings are uprooted from the nursery beds and replanted in waterlogged fields in February.

Opposite: In the cool season months of November and December the hills around Mae Hong Son burst into colour as wild Mexican sunflowers come into bloom. The sight attracts many tourists from Bangkok and Chiang Mai.

A Brief History of Chiang Mai and Northern Thailand

In the late 13th century, much of what we know today as northern Thailand together with some parts of Myanmar and Laos comprised the Lanna kingdom.

Land of a Million Rice Fields

Thais are part of the larger Tai peoples who had been migrating into the area from China since the seventh century. Thais succeeded in taking Hariphunchai, or present-day Lamphun, from the Mon in 1238 and went on to create the independent kingdom of Sukhothai under the rule of King Si Intharathit. In 1296, Chiang Mai or 'new city' was established by King Mengrai (1238–1317) who also formed an alliance with Sukhothai to create the Lanna kingdom (sometimes referred to as Lanna Tai). Known as the 'land of a million rice fields', Lanna extended its influence from Kamphaengphet Province in the south, north to Luang Prabang in what is now Laos, and west into Myanmar. Prior to the creation of Chiang Mai, nearby Wiang Khum Kham was the northern capital. Situated some five kilometres (three miles) south-east of present-day Chiang Mai, it was destroyed by flooding in 1294 but the ruins can still be visited. In Chiang Mai, many reminders of the city's past glories remain including Wat Chiang Man which dates from 1296. Built by King Mengrai, the main hall was constructed using huge teak pillars and houses two ancient and revered Buddha images.

Left: Just outside Chiang Mai are the ruins of Wiang Khum Kham, a former capital that was abandoned due to flooding. A pleasant morning can be spent exploring the site by pony and trap.

Opposite: The chedi at Wat Chiang Man is decorated with images of elephants. Although it has been rebuilt and restored many times over the years, there has been a temple here since 1296, making it the oldest in Chiang Mai.

At the height of its power in the 15th century, Chiang Mai wielded great cultural and religious influence throughout the region. However, its dominance began to wane. A century earlier, the kingdom of Lan Xang (of which Luang Prabang was the capital) had taken territory from Lanna including the city of Chiang Saen on the banks of the Mekong River. Further losses were suffered in 1556 but this time it was Burmese troops who sacked Chiang Mai and maintained their rule until 1774 when the Thais eventually mustered enough force to repel the invaders. It was not until 1804 that the last toehold of the Burmese was overcome and Chiang Saen was retaken from Laos. The legacy of the Burmese occupation is still clearly visible today in the art and architecture of Chiang Mai and is also evident in the local cuisine.

During the 19th century, Chiang Mai could only be reached by a slow and arduous river journey and remained an independent state. In his book 'Half a Century among the Siamese and Lao', Daniel McGilvary (1828-1911), the first American Presbyterian missionary to reach Chiang Mai, stated that the journey took him three months. In 1867, he established the Lao Mission and played a leading role in socio-cultural changes in the north including education and healthcare. To this day Chiang Mai has a sizeable Christian community and many of the hill tribes who were targeted by missionary zeal are Christian.

British companies operating in Myanmar, formerly known as Burma, secured teak concessions for northern Thailand in the mid-1800s when King Mongkut (Rama IV) approved the 'Treaty of Friendship and Commerce' with Sir John Bowring, Britain's representative for Queen Victoria. Similar treaties followed with the USA and several European nations but it was the British Bombay Burmah Corporation that profited most from the deals. However, overlapping concessions, banditry, the murders of British subjects involved in logging and the fear that the British would attempt to gain control of the region forced Bangkok to take control of Chiang Mai and the north in the 1890s.

In the reign of King Rama VI, the first railway line from Bangkok to the north of Thailand was completed. Lampang station opened in 1916 and in 1922 the extension of the line to Chiang Mai was completed. It was a move that made access to the north easy and fuelled the further development of Chiang Mai.

Above: In the north of Thailand there are many statues of King Mengrai, the monarch credited with establishing the cities of Chiang Rai and Chiang Mai. Locals regularly make offerings of flowers and incense in front of the images.

Right: The ancient Buddha images at Wiang Khum Kham are still decorated with robes and worshipped by Thai visitors.

Below right: Wooden panels in the Anantara Resort in Chiang Rai are decorated with distinctive Lanna-style paintings portraying an idealized lifestyle of yesteryear.

The North Today

Today, with its excellent network of roads and highly developed tourist industry, it's easy to believe that northern Thailand, like Chiang Mai, has long-since been an easy destination to explore. Yet it was only in the mid-70s that Roy Hudson wrote in his guide to the region about the road from Chiang Mai to Pai:

> 'Don't try the Pai route. No regular vehicles of any kind traverse this area. It is impassable in the wet even with 4-wheel drive. Motorcycles, however, can make it. A beautiful trip but not yet for the average traveller.'

These words are testament to just how much and how quickly the area has changed. Even in the 90s Pai was a small and seldom-visited backwater. With the onset of Thailand's soufflé economy in 1997, however, a sprinkling of Bangkok's young and trendy headed north opening coffee shops and guesthouses in the town. Today it could be more accurately described as the 'Koh Samui of the north'. Likewise Mae Hong Son, once an isolated Tai Yai community in a remote valley, is now one of Thailand's most charming destinations and Chiang Rai has blossomed into a colourful city with a unique northern character.

History lovers can explore the Chiang Mai National Museum and see a collection of ancient Buddha images, pottery and other important northern Thai relics. On the outskirts of the city the Tribal Museum also offers valuable insights into the hill tribes in the Chiang Mai region and their way of life.

The People

As you might expect in an area bordered by Laos and Myanmar and with China lying further north, the population of Chiang Mai and northern Thailand reflects the historical influences of these countries.

Khon Mueang

The people of the north refer to themselves as 'Khon Mueang' or the 'people of the principalities'. The Khon Mueang are part of the large group of Tai-speaking peoples and as such are closely related to the Lao people in Laos and northeastern Thailand, the Tai Lue from Yunnan, and the Shan from Myanmar. The Tai people throughout the region became known for wet-rice cultivation and farming in the many fertile lowland valleys. Although there are regional differences in traditional dress and dialects, the Khon Mueang are today united by a common language known as 'kham mueang', or the 'language of the principalities', Buddhism, and a distinctive culture and cuisine that are found throughout Chiang Mai, Lampang, Lamphun and Chiang Rai as well as the provinces of Phrae, Phayao and Nan. In recent years, as Chiang Mai and the north have prospered, the people have confidently expressed their identity through art, architecture, and colourful festivals and other celebrations.

Tribal Diversity

For many visitors, the attraction of the north is the discovery of the many hill tribes that inhabit the upland areas. There are seven major tribes; the Akha, Hmong, Karen, Lawa, Lahu, Lisu and Yao. Other smaller groups include the Kamu, Mlabri, Htin and Palong. The tribes are skilled farmers and are also renowned for their craftwork, such as weaving, silverwork and basketry. However, many of the young have turned their back on the traditional way of life and the clothing that identifies each group and have moved to Chiang Mai where they sell crafts or work in restaurants and hotels. The women are more likely to be seen in traditional dress than the men.

The Karen originated in Myanmar and are perhaps the most well integrated of the ethnic tribes. The description hill tribe is a slight misnomer as the majority of the 300,000 population now occupies the lowland areas where they practise wet-rice cultivation and farming. Traditionally the Karen are skilled weavers and wear brightly coloured tunics. Unmarried women wear long, white, v-neck tunics The second largest hill tribe group is the Hmong, often referred to as the Meo, although they consider it derogatory. Originally from western China, the Hmong and sub-groups are present in northern Thailand, Laos, Myanmar and Vietnam. Once known for opium cultivation, the Hmong now grow cash crops, such as cabbages, potatoes, tomatoes and strawberries. The Hmong are animist and use village shamans to commune with the spirit world. The women are renowned for their exquisite needlework and wear heavily embroidered pleated skirts. The men wear baggy black pants with embroidered cuffs.

The Akha are one of the most fiercely independent of the hill tribes. They are also considered the most impoverished, a result of their reluctance to integrate into wider society. They originated in Tibet and are present in China, Laos and Myanmar. The women wear brightly coloured, embroidered tunics and leggings together with elaborate headwear. Today, the Akha supplement their meagre income from highland farming by selling crafts to tourists.

Originally from eastern Tibet, the Lisu tribe settled in the mountains around Chiang Mai, Mae Hong Son and Chiang Rai over 80 years ago. The Lisu are mostly animists and practise ancestor worship but some were converted to Christianity by missionaries. The women wear a knee-length tunic of brightly coloured fabrics. During New Year celebrations in January or February, the women dress in all their finery including lots of silver jewellery.

The Lahu, also known as the Muser, are found in the mountains near the border with Myanmar. Originally from south-west China, they are formed of five sub-groups, namely the Red, Yellow, Black and White Lahu, and Lahu Sheleh. Black Lahu women wear long black jackets with cream stripes and sleeves decorated in bold colours. Their traditional belief system is animist but some have converted to Christianity.

The Yao, also called the Mien, number over 40,000 in Thailand and are mainly found in Chiang Rai, Nan and Phayao Provinces. It is thought that the Yao migrated from southern China in the 19th century. Their written language is a form of modified Chinese and is used to record tribal rituals and history. The women wear loose-fitting black or indigo trousers and a black turban-like headdress. The most distinctive feature, however, is a red ruff attached to the collar of their tunic.

The Lawa are thought to be the first people to inhabit the Chiang Mai valley. Although many are now part of mainstream Thai society, there are Lawa villages in the Mae La Noi and Mae Chaem areas where they cultivate wet rice and grow vegetables. The language is part of the Mon-Khmer group and they are thought to have migrated to Thailand from Cambodia centuries ago. The women wear a short sarong, black leggings and are adorned with strings of red beads around the neck.

Above: An Akha woman wearing her ornate hat and necklaces. The majority of the Akha in Thailand live in the mountains of Chiang Rai Province.

Above centre: An Akha girl, cheeks blushed with rouge, in the market at Tachilek on the border with Myanmar.

Above right: Women of the Yao tribes wear black clothing trimmed with a thick red ruff. There are several Yao villages in the hills of Chiang Rai and Mae Hong Son Provinces.

Opposite: Two Lisu women outside their house wearing colourful traditional clothes. The Lisu are one of several distinctive tribes in the north, many of whom make a living as farmers or by selling crafts.

The Shan and Other Groups

The roots of the Shan, or Tai Yai as they are also known, are in Yunnan, China, from where they migrated into Myanmar. About 30,000 Shan live in Thailand, mainly in Mae Hong Son Province which borders Myanmar and the Shan State. The fact that the area remained relatively isolated for many years has undoubtedly served to protect the Shan culture and give the area a unique ethnic flavour. The Shan are predominately Buddhist and their temples can be distinguished by the elaborately tiered roofs. Shan women also have a liking for *tanaka*, a yellow face powder that acts as a sunscreen made from the bark of a tree.

In Chiang Mai and throughout the major northern towns there are also groups of Haw Chinese Muslims who originally came from Yunnan.

Food

Whereas the cuisine of Thailand's northeast has found popularity throughout the country, northern food is less common outside the region. However, it is incredibly popular with Thai visitors and few leave without bags full of local delicacies.

Northern Soul Food

Of all the wonderfully exotic foods in northern Thailand *kao soi* is the most famous. A dish of deceptive simplicity, it is capable of warming the soul when the cool season mornings begin to bite, can lift your spirits when the rains have dampened them and, as the mercury rises and the air is thick and heavy, it sends out a clear signal that you can handle the heat. In fact a local adage even goes as far as to say that you haven't really been to Chiang Mai unless you have eaten the local *kao soi*. The dish is a rich curry soup containing either pork or chicken ladled over a nest of egg noodles to serve. Condiments include pickled cabbage, lime, red onion and *nahm prik pao* (roasted chilli paste).

Other delights include *sai oua*, a local pork sausage often served in restaurants as 'Chiang Mai hors d'oeuvres' along with northern classics, such as *nahm prik num*, a roasted chilli dip, *kairb moo*, crispy pig skin, and *nahm prik ong*, a delicious pork and tomato dish.

Gaeng hang lay is another well-known northern dish, although its roots are in Myanmar. This mild but richly flavoured pork curry is a firm favourite with locals and visitors. Unlike the cuisine of central Thailand, northern Thai curries seldom use coconut milk and are generally packed with vegetables, making them a much healthier choice. *Gaeng kare* is a classic curry of pork or chicken with a selection of local vegetables including edible flowers. Other favourites include *gaeng khanun*, a curry made using a young and unripe jackfruit and the salad *tam khanun*.

Khanom jeen naam ngeow is a particularly northern way of eating fermented rice noodles. A northern style curry is ladled over the noodles and topped with fresh bean sprouts, cabbage and pickled vegetables.

Left: Northern Thai food is less well known to foreigners than that of the central region but is worth discovering. Pictured here are 'yam hua plee' or banana flower salad (top), a rich Burmese-influenced pork curry called 'gaeng hang lay' (centre right), 'nahm prik num' or roasted chilli dip (centre left), 'gaeng kare', a spicy curry with foraged vegetables (bottom right), and 'tam khanun', a salad made with unripe jackfruit (bottom left).

Opposite: 'Kao soi' noodle soup is a classic, must-try Chiang Mai dish. Here it is shown with condiments of lime, shallots and pickled vegetables, and a plate of 'sai oua', a popular northern Thai sausage.

Right: *Typically, diners order several dishes of northern Thai cuisine which are served at the same time rather than as a succession of course as in Europe. Sticky rice or 'kao neaw' is the preferred rice in the north.*

Opposite page : *Rural northern towns and villages have many fabulous fresh markets to explore. Produce is often bought twice daily, in the early morning and late afternoon. Tomatoes, baby aubergines and 'bu kuang' (a plant used in northern Thai curries to impart a slightly sour flavour) are temptingly displayed (top left).*

Local Fresh Markets

Exploring the fresh food markets in Chiang Mai is a great way to get a bit of a feel for the local way of life. If you want to learn more, then join a guided food walk from Elliebum Boutique Hotel. The two best fresh markets in the old town are Chiang Mai Gate and Somphet. At Ton Lamyai, a fresh flower market by the river, most of the flowers are sold by hill tribe people who grow them in the surrounding mountains.

Cookery schools have flourished in Chiang Mai. Learning to produce a selection of Thai classics is a good way to spend a morning and an excellent way to take home more than memories. Most schools follow a similar formula which begins with a visit to the local market to familiarize students with ingredients followed by a return to the school where participants learn to cook several dishes before tucking into them at a group meal.

Festivals and Events

The residents of Bor Sang, known to visitors as the umbrella village, celebrate their traditional skills at an annual fair in January. They hold a variety of contests and exhibitions, and a 'Miss Bor Sang' pageant. Many stalls also sell the beautiful umbrellas and other locally made handicrafts. The umbrellas are made from brightly coloured *saa* paper derived from the bark of the paper mulberry tree. They have been made in the area around Bor Sang for centuries and many people here still earn a living from making and selling intricately painted examples.

Below: The annual Shan festival of Poi Sang Long or 'precious gems' remains one of Thailand's most colourful and authentic festivals.

Precious Gems

Each year in March or April at Mae Hong Son and the surrounding villages, the Shan or Tai Yai people hold the colourful festival of Poi Sang Long. The event is held to ordain young Shan boys into the monkhood and begins at the temple with the ritual shaving of their hair. The following day they are dressed in brightly coloured clothes and paraded through the town on the shoulders of relatives as *sang long* or precious gems.

This page: *Poi Sang Long is held over several days in March or April. When the young boys have been dressed by the family, they take part in a religious ceremony at the local temple and are blessed by Buddhist monks.*

Yi Peng

The Yi Peng is a major event held in Chiang Mai on the night of November's full moon (although in recent years the event has been heavily promoted by the tourism authority and now goes on for several days). The festival is the northern Thai version of Loy Kratong, a time when thousands of locals head down to the river to float small banana-leaf rafts or *kratongs*. Traditionally the *kratongs* are viewed as a way of asking the river's forgiveness; many also believe that the *kratongs* are capable of taking away unhappiness. In the north, *khom loy*, or floating lanterns, are also released into the night sky.

Opposite top right: *In northern Thailand, the festival of Loy Kratong is known as Yi Peng. It is one of the region's biggest celebrations and includes the release of thousands of lanterns into the sky on the night of November's full moon.*

Opposite top left: *At Yi Peng small rafts made from the trunk of a banana palm are floated on the rivers. Today, kratongs made from bread are also popular.*

Below: *People fill their 'kratong' with flowers, a candle and three incense sticks, then make a wish as they release it onto a river, canal or lake.*

Above: In Chiang Mai at Songkran it's all-out war. With even fire hoses used to spray revellers it's impossible to avoid getting drenched.

Songkran New Year Celebrations

Chiang Mai is famous for holding one of the biggest and most raucous Songkran New Year celebrations. In mid-April, visitors flock here in droves for a week-long water fight during which the city virtually grinds to a halt.

Arts and Crafts

Chiang Mai has a well-deserved reputation as the centre of Thailand's arts and crafts industry. In addition to the umbrella-making village of Bor Sang, Baan Tawai is known for wood carving and San Kampaeng for celadon ceramics and silk.

Wua Lai Silver

Within the city, skilled artisans in the Wua Lai district have been producing exquisite silverwork for centuries. The techniques are thought to have been introduced by Burmese and Shan craftsmen during the 13th century. The popularity of silver is evidenced by its use in ceremonies and rituals. Bowls display intricate patterns that tell the story of Buddhism including the legend of Pra Wej Sundorn, or the life of Buddha before enlightenment. Scenes from the Indian epic, the *Ramayana,* and floral patterns are also common in northern Thai silver. The imagery on the bowls is hammered out from the inside to produce the pattern in high-relief, a technique known as *repoussage.*

The crowning achievement of Wua Lai craftsmen and women is Wat Sri Suphan, an exquisite temple which includes a silver *ubosot* or ordination hall.

Handmade Paper

In the Bor Sang district of Chiang Mai, craftsmen and women have been making paper by hand for centuries. The technique uses pulp made from the bark of the paper mulberry tree. Known as *saa* paper, it is crafted into umbrellas, notebooks, cards and wrapping paper.

Other Crafts

Northern Thai artisans are also renowned as skilled potters, woodcarvers and weavers. Most of the crafts found for sale in Bangkok and in the tourist resorts are actually made in villages around Chiang Mai. It is cheaper to buy them at source and there is often more choice.

Above left and right: Pulp used for making 'saa' paper is mixed into a large tank of water and scooped up on mesh-covered wooden frames. These are then left to dry in the sun before the sheets of paper are peeled off.

Right: In San Kampaeng, on the outskirts of Chiang Mai, there are several workshops producing decorative ceramics, such as the large elephant shown here and classic celadon tableware.

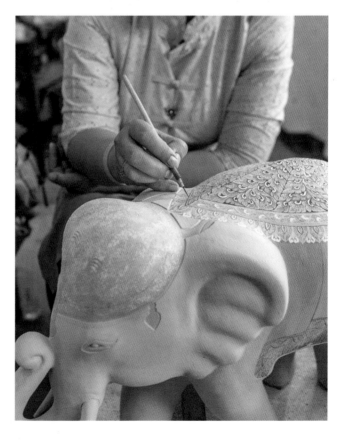

Above: In Bor Sang, several umbrella-making workshops are open to visitors where the artists can be seen making the frames from bamboo and painting the 'saa' paper with intricate designs.

Above left: Situated 15 km (9 miles) from Chiang Mai, Baan Tawai is famous for its wood carvers. There are also many shops selling antique furniture and reproductions in Asian and European styles.

Left: The small hamlet of Mae Chaem, 106 km (66 miles) from Chiang Mai, is renowned for its skilled weavers. Dozens of homes here produce high-quality woven cotton.

Chapter 2: Chiang Mai and Beyond

Steeped in tradition and local culture, the northern city of Chiang Mai is one of Thailand's most appealing provincial capitals. With its own dialect, delicious northern cuisine and unique architectural style, the former kingdom of Lanna – the 'land of a million rice fields'– stands apart from the rest of Thailand. Chiang Mai and the surrounding villages are home to more than 300 temples, including some of the country's most important sacred sites.

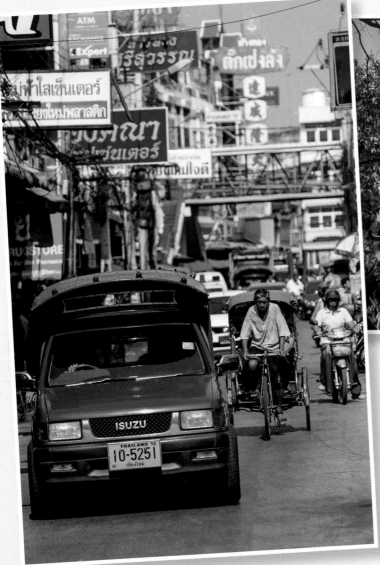

Above: The old quarter of Chiang Mai is framed by a pretty tree-lined moat and the remains of the city walls.

Left: In Chiang Mai, red 'song taews', taxi vans with two benches in the back, ply the streets providing a cheap and easy way to get around.

Opposite: Halfway up Doi Suthep mountain a rest stop provides an opportunity to enjoy panoramic views of the increasingly sprawling city below.

The Ping River

These pages: Along the banks of the Ping River that flows through the middle of Chiang Mai, there are many excellent and popular restaurants serving Thai and international cuisine. It is also possible to take a cruise down the river (above). The old metal bridge or Saphan Lek (opposite top) that spans the Ping River joins the road to Lamphun, which was once the main road into Chiang Mai. The riverbank near the newer Nawarat Bridge (opposite bottom) is a pleasant spot in the evening.

Walking Streets

Rigth: Chiang Mai's popular 'Walking Streets' attract hordes of shoppers who come to browse, buy local products and eat at the vibrant pavement markets from about 4 p.m. until 10 p.m. when the area is pedestrianized. On Saturday evenings, Wua Lai Road is lined with vendors and on Sunday the Tha Pae Gate area and Ratchadamnoen Road pull in the crowds.

San Patong Buffalo Market

Left: The San Patong buffalo market, 25 km (15 miles) from Chiang Mai, is held every Saturday morning from daybreak until midday. Once an integral part of the Thai way of farming life, the water buffalo has been widely replaced by a mechanical cultivator. Less than 20 years ago it was estimated that Thailand was home to ten million working water buffalo. Today the figure is less than 1.5 million and declining rapidly. At the market, visitors can watch local farmers buy and sell the proud beasts, many of which are exported to China.

Wat Chiang Man

Left: Chiang Mai's oldest temple, Wat Chiang Man, can be found on Ratchaphakhinai Road within the city's historic district. The temple was built in 1296 and has been restored in recent years. It's noted for its beautiful chapel with paintings depicting life in a bygone era and a golden chedi with elephant buttresses.

Wat Phra Singh

These pages: Wat Phra Singh is located in the western part of Chiang Mai old town at the end of Ratchadamnoen Road. The temple houses the much revered Phra Buddha Sihing which dates back to the early 1400s and also features exquisite wood carving.

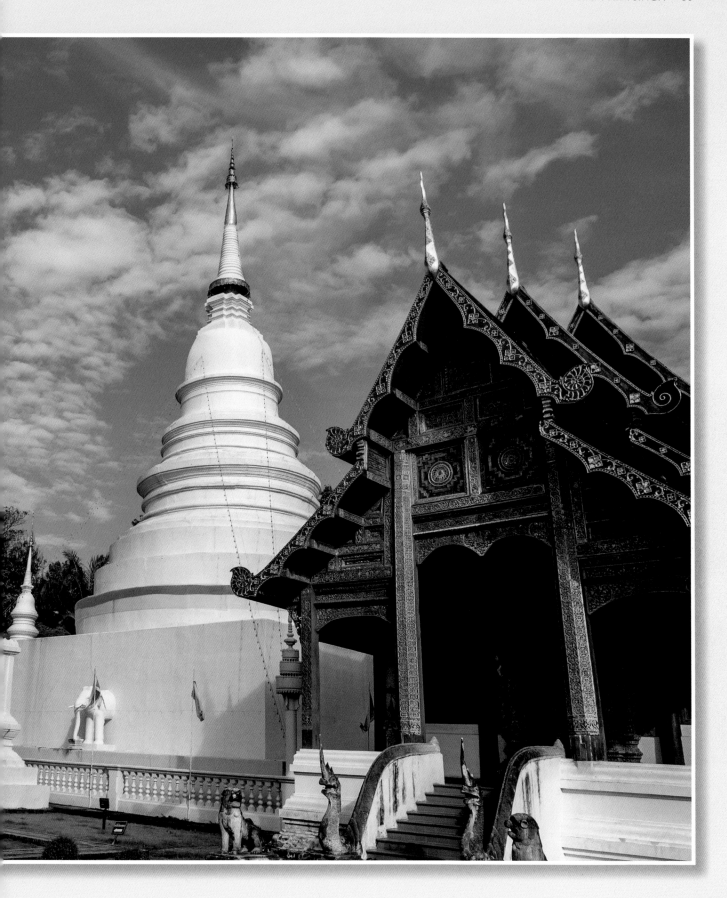

Wat Umong Suan Puthatham

These pages: Hidden away on a tree-covered hillside off Suthep Road, Wat Umong Suan Puthatham, more commonly referred to as Wat Umong, is a 700-year-old forest temple. Wat Umong's most interesting features are the atmospheric forest scattered with Buddha images and the unusual underground tunnels. The latter are used as peaceful retreats for meditation and are dotted with shrines.

Wat Chedi Luang

These pages: *Built by King Saen Muang Ma at the end of the 14th century to enshrine the remains of his father, Wat Chedi Luang's 82-m (269-ft) chedi was partly destroyed by a powerful earthquake in 1545. It was partially reconstructed in the 1990s. The temple once housed the revered Emerald Buddha before it was moved to Bangkok. Today, the 'vihaan' or assembly hall includes an impressive standing Buddha (opposite) known as Phra Chao Attarot.*

Wiang Khum Kham

These pages: The former capital under the rule of King Mengrai (1238–1317), Wiang Khum Kham was abandoned in 1294 due to frequent flooding. Located just a short distance from Chiang Mai, it is now a historical park that includes more than 30 architectural sites. Wat Chedi Liem (below and opposite top) is the main temple within the expansive site and is still used as a place of worship. An enjoyable hour or so can be spent exploring the ruins by pony and trap.

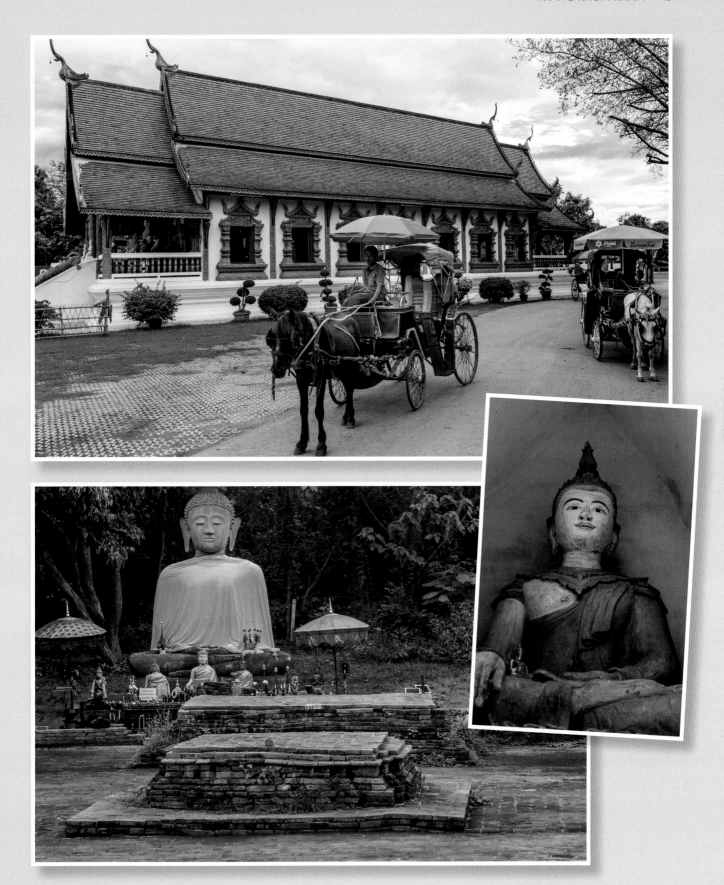

Wat Phra That Doi Suthep

These pages: Doi Suthep is a 1,676-m (5,500-ft) peak that overlooks Chiang Mai. It is also home to the famous temple Wat Phra That Doi Suthep, reached by ascending a stairway of 300 steps. The temple provides spectacular views across the city and surrounding countryside.

Visitors to the temple walk around the chedi several times as an act of worship before leaving offerings of lotus flowers and incense at a Buddha image.

Around Chiang Mai

Chiang Mai is an excellent base from which to explore the surrounding area and there are many attractions for day trips. Historic Lamphun can be reached along an old tree-lined road while the mountainous Mae Rim-Samoeng road is best travelled by car or motorcycle.

Mae Rim, the Mae Sa Valley and Samoeng

These pages: North of the city, the district of Mae Rim, the Mae Sa Valley and Samoeng are linked by a scenic winding road lined with orchid farms, resorts, restaurants, an elephant camp and the picturesque Queen Sirikit Botanical Gardens.

Lamphun

These pages: Once known as Hariphunchai, Lamphun is one of Thailand's oldest towns, believed to have been founded in the mid-ninth century. Lying just 20 km (12½ miles) south of Chiang Mai and reached by a tree-lined road (right), the town's most significant feature is Wat Phra That Hariphunchai, a temple with a 46-m (151-ft) golden chedi (far right) and many beautiful Buddha images (below).

Chapter 3: The Mae Hong Son Loop

Despite the many attractions in the city and its environs, the true beauty of northern Thailand is to be found in the mountains. A popular scenic route is the Mae Hong Son Loop, a 600-km (373-mile) winding drive through some of the country's most impressive scenery. The road from Chiang Mai to Mae Hong Son and onward to Mae Sariang is nothing short of spectacular, boasting 1,864 bends as it winds through the thrilling mountainous terrain. It is understandably popular with adventure motorcyclists and 4-wheel-drive enthusiasts who also take advantage of the numerous dirt trails that lead off into more remote areas. Jeeps and motorcycles are cheap and easy to hire in Chiang Mai. Major stopping points along the way include the towns of Pai, Mae Hong Son and Mae Sariang. The journey makes for a fabulous week-long adventure.

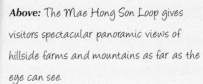

Above: The Mae Hong Son Loop gives visitors spectacular panoramic views of hillside farms and mountains as far as the eye can see.

Left: The weekly morning market at Soppong attracts hill tribe peoples who come to sell fresh produce and buy essentials.

Opposite: Away from the main road and accessed by red dirt tracks are many hill tribe villages. Once transient slash-and-burn farmers, tribes such as the Lisu and Lahu now have a settled lifestyle.

Mae Hong Son

This page: The far northern outpost of Mae Hong Son is a scenic and vibrant town surrounded by rugged terrain. The townspeople are predominately Shan, also referred to as Tai Yai, and local temple architecture shows the strong influence they have exerted over the region in the past. Hill tribe people scattered in small villages throughout the mountains and frequently seen in the town's markets, include Karen, Lisu, Lahu and Hmong. Mae Hong Son is one of the country's premier destinations for trekking and less strenuous activities, such as kayaking and rafting or cave exploration.

This page: Many of the temples in Mae Hon Song reflect the strong Burmese influence. Wat Phra That Doi Kong Mu, perched upon a hilltop and overlooking the town, is a fine example and has two lavishly decorated chedis. Wat Jong Kham and Wat Jong Klang, next to the scenic lake in the town centre (below), are both interesting examples of Burmese-style temples. Wat Jong Klang was established over 200 years ago by the Shan.

Right: In the evenings the road around the lake in Mae Hong Son is lined with food stalls where visitors can sit and sample local dishes while enjoying a view of the brightly lit Wat Jong Kham and Wat Jong Klang.

Pai

Right: East of Mae Hong Son, the town of Pai has become a haven for backpackers and offers everything from trekking, rafting and elephant camps to massage, hot springs and yoga, but has lost much of its former charm to mass tourism.

Doi Inthanon

This page: Located in Chiang Mai Province, Doi Inthanon National Park is the home of Thailand's highest mountain. The doi or mountain peak is 2,565 m (8,415 ft) high and lies at the heart of a 48,240 hectare (119,200 acre) national park. During the coolest month of January, a light frost is not uncommon. Just short of the summit are two chedis built to honour the 60th birthdays of the late King Bhumibol and his wife, Queen Sirikit.

Soppong

These pages: The town of Soppong, also known as Pangmapha, attracts adventure travellers who come to explore the area's many caves and to trek in the mountains. The most famous cave is Tam Lod. The enormous chambers can be explored by raft with the aid of a local guide and lantern. At dusk, thousands of swallows can be seen entering the cave to roost as an equally impressive number of bats leave for their night flight. At the lovely Little Eden Guesthouse a bamboo suspension bridge spans the river (top right). Hill tribe women can also be seen in the nearby local market (below).

Mae Sariang

These pages: Sitting at the south-western corner of the Mae Hon Song loop is Mae Sariang. Visitors to the town can drive 50 km (31 miles) through beautiful countryside to Mae Sam Laeb on the banks of the Salween River, which separates Thailand from Myanmar. From here, when conditions in Myanmar are peaceful, boat trips can be taken up the river and the hills explored on foot.

Chapter 4: Chiang Rai and the Golden Triangle

The northern city of Chiang Rai sits at the heart of one of the country's most rural provinces. Mountainous and bordered in the north-east by the mighty Mekong River, Chiang Rai Province is a playground for those seeking adventure and stunning scenery.

Although Chiang Rai and the surrounding area can be visited year-round, it is undoubtedly at its best during the cool season from November until February when it is more comfortable to go trekking in the hills. It is also possible to arrange boat rides to small but interesting towns and hamlets along the Kok River. Ethnic groups living in the province include Karen, Lisu, Lahu, Akha, Hmong and Yao.

The infamous Golden Triangle, known locally as Sop Ruak, is where the borders of Laos, Myanmar and Thailand converge. Once an area notorious for opium cultivation and trading, the Golden Triangle now attracts thousands of visitors each year.

Chiang Rai

This page: Known as the Gateway to the Golden Triangle, the city of Chiang Rai lies in a fertile valley 180 km (112 miles) north of Chiang Mai. The town has a less commercial feel than Chiang Mai and consequently a more relaxed atmosphere. Although the town itself has limited attractions, it's a good place for a couple of night's rest and relaxation, and an excellent base for treks into the surrounding hills.

Right: The amazing 'Baan Dam' or 'Black House' built by Thai artist, Thawan Duchanee. This expansive compound, which is open to the public, is full of buildings and exhibits created by the late artist.

Wat Rong Khun

Left and above: One of Chiang Rai's most spectacular attractions is Wat Rong Khun. This beautiful temple is the on-going work of the renowned Thai artist, Chalermchai Kositpipat, and skilfully blends traditional Buddhist art with modern concepts. The unique building is entirely white and decorated with thousands of pieces of mirrored glass. Inside it contains murals, paintings and Buddha images. Wat Rong Khun is particularly impressive on the night of a full moon.

Rai Mae Fah Luang Art and Cultural Park

Left: Established under the patronage of the late Princess Mother, the Rai Mae Fah Luang Art and Cultural Park houses a collection of northern Thai religious and secular art and artefacts. The buildings are set in beautiful landscaped gardens.

Wat Archa Thong

Above: Wat Archa Thong, or the Temple of the Golden Horse, was established by an ex-Thai boxer turned Buddhist monk to help care for and educate orphans. The temple is also renowned for its many horses and for the monks who collect alms on horseback in the morning.

Doi Mae Salong

This page: A comfortable day trip from Chiang Rai, Doi Mae Salong is covered with tea plantations. Visitors can see tea being picked and processed and sample the Chinese-style brews.

Doi Tung Development Project

This page: The Doi Tung Development Project began as a royal initiative to help eradicate opium cultivation, drug use and rural poverty by offering villagers a practical and sustainable alternative. They now grow vegetables, coffee and flowers, as well as make and sell crafts, such as woven textiles. At the summit of Doi Tung visitors can visit Phra That Doi Tung, a chedi that was constructed in 911 AD. and one of the oldest and most sacred sites in northern Thailand (centre). There are also beautiful gardens dedicated to the late Princess Mother (above and below).

Sop Ruak

Right and below: *The actual Golden Triangle (Sop Ruak) is nine kilometres (five and a half miles) from Chiang Saen, at the confluence of the Mekong and Ruak Rivers.*

Chiang Saen

Right: *Once an important city in the Lanna kingdom, today Chiang Saen is scattered with ancient ruins, such as Wat Pa Sak (pictured). The temple dates from the 13th century and includes a 13.5-m (44-ft) chedi with Buddha images in recesses around the base.*

Anantara Elephant Camp and Resort

This page: The luxurious Anantara Golden Triangle Elephant Camp and Resort offers guests a unique learning experience at its traditional mahout village. The inspirational camp works alongside the Golden Triangle Asian Elephant Foundation to provide elephants with a safe and caring environment.

Mae Sai

Left and below: Mae Sai is 62 km (38½ miles) north of Chiang Rai and makes for an interesting day trip or overnight stop. This busy trading post is on the border with Myanmar and linked to it by a bridge. When the situation in Myanmar is peaceful, it is possible to cross here to visit the vibrant market town of Tha Khi Lek for the day.

Chiang Khong

Right: At the town of Chiang Khong, travellers can cross the Fourth Thai-Lao Friendship Bridge over the Mekong River and enter Laos at Huai Xai or take a boat down the Mekong to Luang Prabang.

Phu Chi Fah

This page: Phu Chi Fah is a mountain 25 km (15½ miles) north of Doi Pha Thang, the summit of which offers a spectacular viewpoint of the surrounding area. It is extremely popular in the cool season when Thai tourists flock to the peak to watch the sun rise over a sea of early morning mist.

Chapter 5: East of Chiang Mai

The first train from Bangkok to Lampang arrived in 1916 and was instrumental in opening up the north to commerce. The line was later extended to Chiang Mai. Northeast of Lampang lies Phayao and Nan, two easygoing provincial towns surrounded by bucolic countryside.

Lampang

This page: Renowned for its horse-drawn carriages, Lampang is a popular destination for daytrippers from Chiang Mai. It lies just 100 km (62 miles) to the south-east.

Phayao

This page: Situated beside a picturesque lake, Phayao is the ideal place to break the journey between Chiang Mai and Nan. Lakeside guesthouses, bars and restaurants benefit from sunset views. The fertile valleys around Phayao are carpeted with rice fields. Teams of villagers come together to help with planting and harvest.

Nan

These pages: Bordering Laos, the rural province of Nan is attracting an ever-increasing number of visitors who come to enjoy the scenery and northern culture. In the town of Nan there are several beautiful temples to discover (top), and evening and morning fresh markets with a wide variety of northern cuisine (below). The nearby Doi Phu Kha National Park includes several 2,000-m (6,500-ft) peaks and winding mountain roads (opposite).

Getting About

Chiang Mai lies 800 km (500 miles) north of Bangkok and an hour away by air. The city is served by several airlines. Lampang, Mae Hong Son, Chiang Rai and Nan are also connected by regular flights.

Right: In some northern towns 'samlors' or tricycle taxis can still be seen. They are popular with the older generation of locals and tourists. Fares are negotiated before the journey starts.

Opposite: 'Song taews', literally 'two benches' because of the two long wooden seats in the back, are one of the most common forms of transport in Chiang Mai and the surrounding area. Different coloured 'song taews' serve specific routes for a set fare of just a few baht.

The overnight train from Bangkok's Krungthep Aphiwat station to Chiang Mai makes for an interesting and usually cheaper travel option, taking 12 hours in total. En route, trains stop at Den Chai (for buses to Nan), Lampang and Lamphun. The air-conditioned carriages are comfortable and some trains also feature a restaurant car. Be sure to book in advance and ask for a bottom bunk. They are wider and more comfortable than the upper bunks.

Mostly overnight, air-con buses link Bangkok's Northern Bus Terminal with all the towns mentioned in this book, which in turn are connected to each other by a network of local buses.

Chiang Mai is not a particularly easy place to get around. Visitors can use the ubiquitous *tuk-tuks* but agree a price before embarking on your journey. Online taxi services such as Grab are also available. The hundreds of red *song taews* (pick-up truck taxis) that drive around charge a flat fee of 30 baht when acting as share taxis. *Song taews* of other colours travel routes beyond the city.

Undoubtedly the best way to travel around town is on a scooter. Several scooter and car hire shops are scattered along Moonmuang Rd. Northern Wheels on Chaiyaphum Road is one of the best and most reliable car hire firms in the town.

An excellent road map of the area is published by GT-Rider and is widely available in Chiang Mai. The best information regarding motorcycle touring in the north of Thailand is on the website www.gt-rider.com.

Resources

Northern Wheels

70/4-8 Chaiyaphum Road, Chiang Mai, Tel 053 874478
www.northwheels.com

Adventure Tours, Including Trekking, Cycling, Nature Tours and Kayaking

Contact Travel, Thasala, Chiang Mai, Tel 081 681 2400
www.active-thailand.com

Chiang Mai Thai Cookery School

47/2 Moon Muang Road (opp. Tha Phae Gate), Chiang Mai,
Tel 053 206388
www.facebook.com/CMTCS1993

Guided Food Walks in Chiang Mai

Elliebum Boutique Hotel, 114/3–5 Ratchamankha Road,
Chiang Mai, Tel 090 318 6429
www.facebook.com/elliebumboutiquehotel

References

McGilvary, Daniel. 2001. *A Half Century Among the Siamese and the Lao*. White Lotus

Andrew Forbes and David Henley. 1997. *Khon Muang: people and principalities of north Thailand*. Teak House

Christian Goodden.1999. *Around Lanna – a guide to Thailand's northern border region*. Jungle Books

Mick Shippen. 2005. *Traditional Ceramics of South East Asia*. A&C Black

Acknowledgements

Thanks to Floyd Cowan from Asian Journeys magazine, Esther de la Cruz at Balcony Media Group, Stefan Noll at The Chedi Chiang Mai, Mark Thomson at Anantara Hotels, Resorts & Spas, and Phen Bidasak, northern Thailand's best trekking guide and owner of the delightful Little Eden Guesthouse in Mae Hong Son Province: www.littleeden-guesthouse.com.

About the Author

Mick Shippen is a freelance writer and award-winning photographer who has been based in Southeast Asia for 15 years. He travels extensively throughout Asia conducting research for articles and taking photographs for local and international newspapers and magazines.

He is the author of five other titles in this series: *Enchanting Cambodia, Enchanting Laos, Enchanting Thailand, Enchanting Myanmar, Enchanting Bangkok,* and *The Traditional Ceramics of South East Asia*. He has provided content and images for several leading guidebooks, and his work has also appeared in numerous magazines, the *Bangkok Post,* and the *Australian Sunday Telegraph*.

His images are represented by Gallery Stock www.gallerystock.com. Images can be viewed at www.mickshippen.com

Index

ASIA
BOOKS

Published and Distributed in Thailand by Asia Books Co., Ltd.,
88/9 Soi Samanchan-Barbos, Prakanong, Klongtoey, Bangkok 10110, Thailand
Tel: (66) 2-146-599; Email: information@asiabooks.com
www.asiabooks.com

This edition published in the United Kingdom in 2024 by John Beaufoy Publishing,
11 Blenheim Court, 316 Woodstock Road, Oxford OX2 7NS, England
www.johnbeaufoy.com

ISBN 978-1-913679-56-9

Designed by Glyn Bridgewater
Cover design by Ginny Zeal
Cartography by William Smuts
Project management by Rosemary Wilkinson

Printed and bound in Malaysia by Times Offset (M) Sdn. Bhd.

Photo credits: Anantara Chiang Mai Restort (p.5 bottom); Shutterstock/Koryaprincess (p.26),
Pickauaung (p.34,) Pungu x (p.56, bottom), KoBoZaa (p.70 bottom)
Front: Wat Phra Singh, Chiang Mai © Shutterstock/Minto.ong Back cover, left to right: Red Lahu girls
in traditional dress at a festival, Bor Sang umbrellas, The colourful festival of Poi Sang Long,
Wild Mexican sunflowers, all © Mick Shippen.

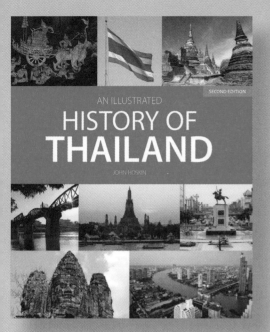
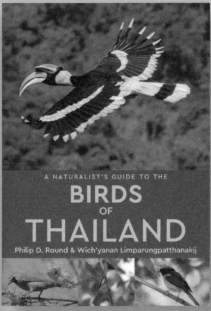
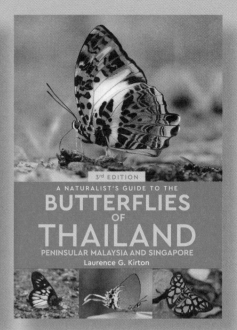

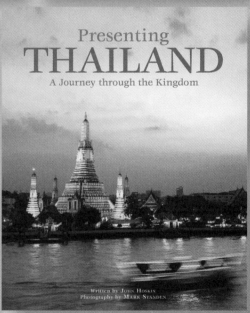